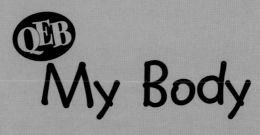

My Body

Why do I wash my hands?

Angela Royston

QEB Publishing

Published in the United States by
QEB Publishing, Inc.
3 Wrigley, Suite A
Irvine, CA 92618

www.qeb-publishing.com

Library of Congress Cataloging-in-Publication Data

Royston, Angela.
  Why do I wash my hands? / Angela Royston.
     p. cm. -- (QEB my body)
  Includes index.
  ISBN 978-1-59566-972-8 (hardcover)
  1. Hygiene--Juvenile literature. I. Title.
  RA777.R694 2010
  613--dc22
                                    2009015228

ISBN 978-1-59566-779-3 (paperback)

Printed and bound in China

Author Angela Royston
Consultant Terry Jennings
Project Editor Judith Millidge
Designer and Picture Researcher
       Louise Downey
Illustrator Chris Davidson

Publisher Steve Evans
Creative Director Zeta Davies
Managing Editor Amanda Askew

Picture credits
(t=top, b=bottom, l=left, r=right, c=center, fc=front
cover)
Corbis Tom Stewart 20
Dorling Kindersley Susanna Price 12b, Andy
Crawford and Steve Gorton 13, 18t
Getty Images Loungepark 5br, Photoshot 18tr,
Jamie Gril 21tl, James Hardy 21b
Shutterstock Larisa Lofitskaya 4, Elena Elisseeva
5t, phdpsx 6b, Robert Spriggs 7b, Suzanne Tucker
7t, Cameramannz 7b, Nassyrov Ruslan 7b, Yummy
8b, tamzinm 8l, Lukacs Racz 8r, Robyn Mackenzie
8c, Ray Hub 8bc, Muriel Lasure 9b, Thomas M
Perkins 9t, ryby 10t, Noam Armonn 11t, Renata
Osinska 11b, Sebastian Kaulitzki 12t, Uravid 12–13,
3445128471 14, Lana Langlois 14b, Yuri Shirokov 14b,
3445128471 17t, Juriah Mosin 19b
Alamy Don Smith 16

Words in **bold** are
explained in the glossary
on page 22.

Contents

Keeping clean

Your hands and skin get dirty from all the things you touch during the day. Your fingers may get sticky with food, and your hands may get grubby from playing indoors or outside.

Children can get dirty every day.

Your skin makes **sweat** to keep you cool. Sweat contains salt and other substances, which are left on your skin after the sweat has dried.

This child is muddy and sweaty from playing soccer.

You need to wash your skin to wash away dirt, sweat, and germs.

Some dirt contains **germs**. These are tiny living things that are too small to see. If they get inside your body, they can make you ill.

5

Amazing skin

Pore

Hair

Sweat

Skin protects your body and keeps out dirt and germs. Skin is **waterproof** and stretchy. Most of your skin is covered with fine hairs.

The hairs on your skin help to keep you warm.

Our skin is waterproof, and so keeps water out of our bodies when we swim or bathe.

Old skin flakes off and is replaced by new skin. If your skin is cut or scraped, your body repairs the damage and new skin grows over the **wound**.

As a scrape heals, new skin grows under the scab.

Activity

Test a piece of cling wrap, a tissue, and a bandage to see which is most like skin. Which one lets you bend your finger most easily? Which ones are waterproof?

7

Washing and drying

The best way to clean your hands is to wet them and rub soap all over them. Then rinse your hands in clean water and dry them carefully on a clean towel.

Towel

Nail brush

Bubble bath

Soap, bubble bath, a nail brush, and a towel can all be used to keep clean.

Hand soap

Activity

Mix some flour and water together with your hands to make a sticky dough. Rinse your hands in cold water. Now clean them using warm water, soap, and a nailbrush. Which way works best?

If dirt gets stuck under your nails, clean them with a nailbrush. Have your nails cut from time to time. Short nails are less likely to get dirty.

Scrubbing your nails with a nailbrush is the best way to clean them.

Clean all over

You should bath or shower regularly so that your skin is clean all over. Otherwise, your skin could become itchy, and your feet might start to smell. Washing gets rid of dirt, sweat, and old skin.

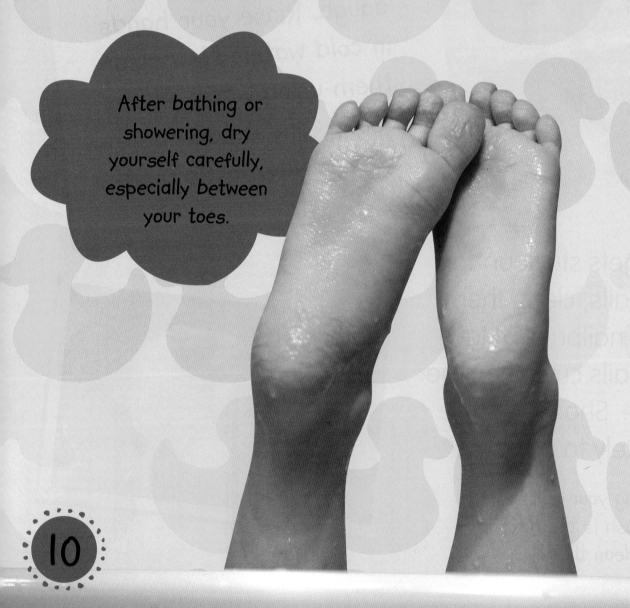

After bathing or showering, dry yourself carefully, especially between your toes.

Activity

Wash and rinse your hair, then run your fingers down a strand of hair. If it squeaks, it is clean. Clean hair is easy to brush.

Wash your hair with shampoo at least once a week. If you don't, your head could become itchy. Conditioner helps to make your hair shiny and easy to comb.

Shampoo cleans your hair and the skin on your head.

11

Bacteria and viruses

Bacteria and **viruses** are different kinds of germs. If they get inside your body, some of them can make you ill.

Usually bacteria are too small to see. This photo shows what bacteria look like.

Activity

Use a hand mirror to look inside your mouth. Can you see any germs? They are there even though you cannot see them. Your saliva will kill most of them.

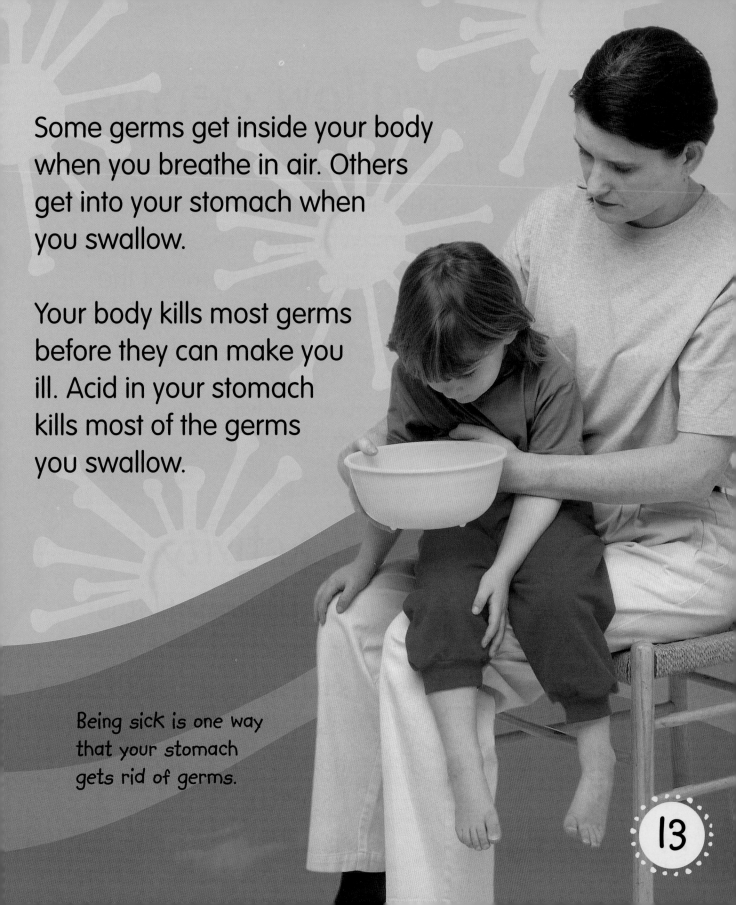

Some germs get inside your body when you breathe in air. Others get into your stomach when you swallow.

Your body kills most germs before they can make you ill. Acid in your stomach kills most of the germs you swallow.

Being sick is one way that your stomach gets rid of germs.

13

Don't swallow germs

If you touch something with germs on, some of the germs will stick to your fingers. When you use your fingers to eat something, some of the germs could go into your mouth, and then into your stomach.

Germs on your hands can rub off onto your food.

Activity

Suck a lollipop until it is sticky. Take it out of your mouth and sprinkle it with some flour. Does it stick to the lollipop? This shows how easily germs stick to things.

14

Keep germs out of your mouth by always washing your hands before you eat. Wash unpeeled fruit before you eat it, too.

Germs on your fingers or food travel from your mouth to your stomach.

1. If there are germs on your fingers, they may be passed to your food, which you put in your mouth.

2. The germs travel down into your stomach.

3. The acid in your stomach kills most of the germs.

15

Flush and wash!

Poo contains millions of germs. These germs stick to surfaces around the toilet. Some of them can get on your hands.

Flushing the toilet helps to wash many of the germs down the drain.

You should always wash your hands after you have used the toilet. If you don't, the germs can move from your hands into your mouth when you eat. These germs can make you sick or give you a bad tummy ache.

Use soap and water to wash your hands well after using the toilet.

Activity

Mix up some powder paint and water. Cover your hands with paint and then press them onto a big sheet of paper. How many handprints can you make? This shows how paint (and germs) cling to your skin.

17

Don't pass on germs

Coughs and colds pass easily from one person to another. When you cough or sneeze, millions of germs shoot into the air. Other people could then breathe in some of your germs.

Sneezing can spread germs in the air.

18

When you blow your nose or sneeze, lots of germs get onto your fingers. You could leave germs on everything you touch. Stop this from happening by using a tissue when you sneeze.

Used tissues should always be thrown away into a covered trash can.

Activity

If you sneeze, cover your nose. If you cough, cover your mouth. Wash your hands, too, so that you do not pass on your germs.

Cuts and scrapes

Germs can also get inside your body if your skin is scratched or broken. If a wound bleeds, the blood helps to wash away germs and dirt. However, you still need to wash the wound carefully.

You may need an adult to help you wash a cut or graze.

When the wound is clean, dry it carefully. Cover it with a bandage to stop germs getting in. Then the wound will begin to heal itself.

A bandage keeps a cut clean until it begins to heal.

Activity

If you scratch or graze your skin, keep a diary of what happens to it as it heals. How long does it take for the scab to fall off?

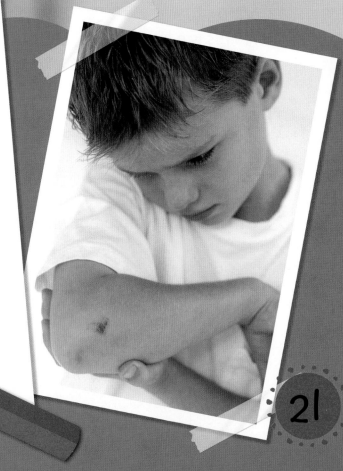

Glossary

Bacteria
Germs are made of tiny bacteria. Bacteria cause illnesses such as ear infections and stomach upsets. Medicines called antibiotics are used to kill bacteria.

Germs
All germs are tiny living things. They are so small that you need a microscope to see them. Germs include bacteria and viruses. They can make you ill if they get inside your body. Germs can pass from one person to another.

Virus
A virus is a kind of germ. Viruses cause illnesses such as colds and flu. Antibiotic medicines do not kill viruses.

Sweat
The salty water that oozes out through tiny holes in your skin when you are hot is called sweat.

Waterproof
Something is waterproof when it does not let any water through it.

Wound
Your body is wounded when your skin is damaged or cut.

Notes for parents and teachers

1. Encourage the children to take an interest in their own health. Talk to them about the importance of washing their hands, particularly before eating and after using the toilet.

2. Make washing more interesting by collecting a selection of fun soaps in different colors, shapes, and smells. Bubble bath makes bathing more fun, too.

3. Experiment with soap bubbles. Run a bowl of warm water and add dishwashing liquid. Agitate the water to make it foamy. Show the children how to make a bubble by rubbing your thumb against your forefinger and then touching the tip of your thumb to the tip of your finger to make a circle of soapy water. Blow the water to form the bubble. Who can make the biggest bubble?

4. Encourage the children to be aware of food hygiene. Show them how to separate uncooked meat, for example, from other food in the refrigerator. Encourage them to check the "use by" dates on food, such as fruit yogurts and smoothies, before eating them.

5. Wash or peel fruit and vegetables, such as apples and carrots, before children eat them. Ask the children to help you to wash grapes, cherries, strawberries, and other fruits.

6. Talk about germs and how small they are. If you are going on a picnic or somewhere where you cannot wash your hands before eating, use antibacterial gel instead.

Index

QEB

My Body

Why Do I Wash My Hands?

Why do we use soap?
Is your skin waterproof?
How do germs pass from one person to another?

Find the answers to these questions and much, much more in this picture-packed introduction to the human body.

What are you waiting for?
Don't sweat it—get reading!

- Close-ups and cutaway diagrams
- Fantastic photographs
- Clear text makes complex ideas easy to understand

ISBN 978-1-59566-779-3

9 781595 667793